INT

They can take the form of … supper, or pancake breakfast … base-
ment or a town hall — whate… church sup-
pers consistently serve up traditional, tasty New England fare.

Decidedly down to earth, church suppers do more than offer town folk a hearty meal and a few hundred dollars for a worthy cause. They provide an excuse for the whole community to come together, teens and great-grandparents, shopkeepers and doctors, conservatives and liberals, in a place where their differences seem to fade and they have a chance to just relax, catch up on each others lives and share a good meal. Breaking bread together seems to help keep a town together. The event also helps to preserve a sense of tradition in a community, a reminder of a common past and a future held together by an event at which the faces change as the decades pass, but tradition is passed on. It is traditions like these that help towns weather the pressures that sometimes threaten to tear them apart.

We don't know when they started, but they've been around as long as anyone around here can remember. The annual appearance of a sign at the front of the church announcing the event is a comforting sight, a reminder that some things don't ever really change, and like spring, the church supper will return year after year.

We have created this cookbook, excerpted from our recently published, *Yankee's Church Supper and Pot Luck Dinner Cookbook*, (Villard Books, available in book stores everywhere), to make sure that in this age of couch potatoes and Internet chat rooms, we don't lose something important: the tradition and connectedness provided by the traditional New England church supper. This book contains some of our favorites from church groups all over New England, and we've also included a chapter of classic church supper fare in quantities to feed a crowd. We've also included tips for putting on a successful church supper (in case you find yourself wanting to start or restart the tradition in your community and you have no one to teach you the ropes). And a table to help you calculate how much soup, spaghetti sauce and coffee you'll need to prepare.

So put on your apron and cook up a tradition. Bon appetit!

YANKEE Magazine

TABLE OF CONTENTS

Soups, Chowders & Stews

Main Dish Minestrone

Yield: 6 to 8 servings

ADAPTED FROM A RECIPE BY JEAN CAIRD, ST. BRENDAN'S CATHOLIC WOMAN'S CLUB, COLEBROOK, NEW HAMPSHIRE

A flavorful soup, made mostly from ingredients already on the kitchen shelf. Serve with a fresh, crusty bread for a hearty meal.

1 tablespoon olive oil
1/2 pound sweet or hot Italian sausage, crumbled
1 large onion, chopped
1 garlic clove, minced
1/2 cup chopped celery
1/2 cup chopped carrot
1/2 cup chopped green bell pepper
1 can (16 ounces) whole tomatoes
4 cups chicken stock or broth
2 cups shredded cabbage
2 tablespoons chopped fresh parsley
1/2 teaspoon dried basil
1 bay leaf
pinch dried thyme
1/2 cup uncooked elbow macaroni
1 cup cooked kidney beans
freshly grated Parmesan cheese *(optional)*

In a large saucepan or stockpot, heat the oil. Add the sausage and cook until browned. Drain off all but 1 tablespoon of the fat. Add the onion, garlic, celery, carrot, and green pepper and sauté until the vegetables are soft, about 5 minutes. Add the tomatoes with their liquid, chicken stock, cabbage, and herbs. Bring to a boil, cover, and simmer for 30 minutes. Add the macaroni and beans and cook until the macaroni is tender, about 30 minutes. Remove the bay leaf before serving. Sprinkle each serving with Parmesan cheese, if desired.

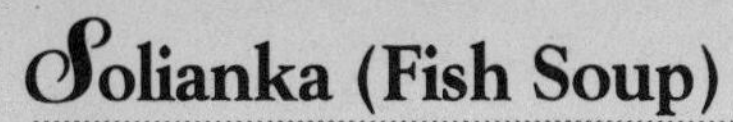

Solianka (Fish Soup)

Yield: 6 to 8 servings

B.W. Amaral, M.D., Boscawen Historical Society, Boscawen, New Hampshire

This soup can be served either slightly warm or piping hot — great for guests at any time of year.

2 cups chopped onions
1 bay leaf
2 to 3 sprigs fresh parsley
3 teaspoons salt
6 cups water
2-1/2 pounds salmon steaks (or substitute halibut or haddock)
4 to 6 tablespoons (1/2 to 3/4 stick) butter
2 medium-size cucumbers, peeled, halved, seeded, and chopped into 1/2-inch cubes
4 tomatoes, peeled, seeded, and coarsely chopped
1 quart clam juice or other fish broth
1/2 teaspoon white pepper
2 tablespoons chopped black olives, rinsed
2 tablespoons chopped fresh parsley, fennel, or cilantro
20 pitted black olives
1 lemon, thinly sliced

In a large saucepan or stockpot, combine 1 cup of the chopped onions, bay leaf, parsley, salt, and water. Cover and bring to a boil over high heat. Add the fish. Reduce the heat and simmer, uncovered, for about 6 minutes, or until the fish is firm to the touch. Remove the fish and cut into 1-inch chunks. Strain the broth through a fine sieve, pressing down on the onions to extract all the juice. Set aside.

Wipe out the saucepan and melt the butter in the pan. Add the remaining 1 cup of chopped onions and sauté until the onions are soft but not brown, about 5 minutes. Then add the cucumbers and tomatoes and simmer for about 10 minutes. Add the reserved fish broth and the 1 quart clam broth or other fish broth, along with the remaining ingredients. Simmer for about 15 minutes. Then add the fish and continue simmering until the fish is warmed through. Serve hot or warm.

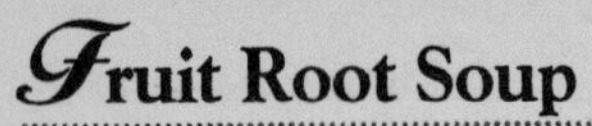

Fruit Root Soup

Yield: 6 servings

Susan Gagnon, Hopkinton Cookie Exchange, Hopkinton, New Hampshire

Inspired by a traditional Finnish recipe, this soup is delicious served either as an appetizer or as a main course with a hearty dark bread and a sharp cheese.

2 tablespoons olive oil
1 medium-size onion, chopped
3 medium-size parsnips, peeled and sliced
4 to 5 medium-size carrots, sliced
1 sweet potato, peeled and sliced
1 ripe pear, peeled, cored, and chopped
2 cans (14 ounces each) chicken or vegetable broth
2 cups water
1/2 cup white wine or apple cider (or juice)
1 teaspoon black pepper
1/4 teaspoon ground cloves
1/4 teaspoon ground nutmeg
1/4 teaspoon ground ginger
1/4 teaspoon ground cumin

In a large saucepan or stockpot, heat the olive oil over medium-high heat. Add the onion, parsnips, carrots, sweet potato, and pear, and sauté for 10 to 15 minutes. Add the broth, water, wine, and all the spices. Simmer for 20 minutes. Let cool slightly, then purée in a food processor or blender until smooth. Serve hot.

Dorset Black Bean Soup

Yield: 8 to 10 servings

Peggy Gilbert, Dorset Historical Society, Dorset, Vermont

A good soup that's low in fat.

1 pound dry black beans
water
6 cups defatted chicken, vegetable, or ham broth
1 bay leaf
1 large or 2 medium-size onions, chopped
1 celery stalk, including leaves, chopped
2 green bell peppers, chopped
1 large tomato, peeled and chopped
1 to 3 garlic cloves, minced

(continued)

6 serrano chili peppers (or to taste)
1 can (6 ounces) tomato paste
1/4 teaspoon hot pepper sauce
1/4 teaspoon black pepper
2 tablespoons Worcestershire sauce
lemon slices, to garnish

Wash the beans. Combine with water to cover in a large saucepan or stockpot and soak overnight.

The next morning, drain the beans. Combine the beans with 2 cups water, the broth, and the bay leaf. Bring to a boil; then reduce the heat and simmer for 1-1/2 hours. Add the remaining ingredients, except the lemon slices, and simmer for 2 hours.

Remove the bay leaf. Blend the soup in a blender for a smooth soup or mash the beans with a potato masher for a chunky soup. Serve hot, garnishing each bowl with a slice of lemon.

Zucchini-Potato Soup

Yield: 8 servings

CORA LAROCHELLE, AUBURN GROUP OF WORCESTER COUNTY EXTENSION SERVICE, AUBURN, MASSACHUSETTS

Very different, very flavorful and very good — a big hit even with those who aren't normally fond of soups.

5 cups chicken broth
1 pound zucchini (4 small), thinly sliced
1 large potato, thinly sliced
1 large onion, thinly sliced
3 eggs
2 tablespoons lemon juice
salt and pepper to taste

In a large saucepan, bring the broth to a boil. Add the zucchini, potato, and onion. Reduce the heat and simmer, covered, for 15 minutes.

In a small bowl, beat the eggs. Add the lemon juice and 1/2 cup of the broth. Stir into the soup. Increase the heat to medium and heat for one minute, stirring constantly; do not boil. Season to taste with salt and pepper and serve immediately. Note: be sure to follow the directions carefully when adding the eggs and lemon juice; otherwise the mixture is likely to curdle.

Cold Strawberry Soup

Yield: 8 to 10 servings

CAROLYN MULLER, ST. PETER'S EPISCOPAL CHURCH, WESTON, MASSACHUSETTS

Cool and refreshing — this soup is a winner during strawberry season.

2 quarts fresh strawberries
1 cup white sugar
2 cups water
1/4 cup fresh lemon juice
grated zest of 1 lemon
2 cups Rhine wine

In a food processor or blender, purée the berries. Set aside.

In a small saucepan, combine the sugar and water. Boil for 10 minutes to make a sugar syrup. Cool.

Add the berries to the cooled syrup. Stir in the lemon juice and zest. Chill well. Just before serving, stir in the wine.

Cream of Broccoli Soup

Yield: 8 to 10 servings

NATALIE MARKO, NEW ENGLAND HISTORIC GENEALOGICAL SOCIETY, BOSTON, MASSACHUSETTS

A wonderful lunch when served with an herb bread and a fruit dessert, this non-puréed soup has plenty of flavor and plenty of texture. If you prefer an even stronger flavor, try substituting a sharper variety for all or part of the cheese.

6 cups water
10 ounces fresh or frozen chopped broccoli
3/4 cup finely chopped onion
2 cups shredded American cheese
2 teaspoons salt
2 teaspoons white pepper
1 teaspoon garlic powder
1 cup milk
1 cup light cream
1/4 cup butter
1/2 cup cold water
1/3 cup all-purpose white flour

(continued)

In a large saucepan, bring the water to a boil. Add the broccoli and onion; boil for 10 to 12 minutes. Add the cheese, salt, pepper, and garlic powder. Cook over medium heat, stirring constantly, until the cheese melts. Add the milk, cream, and butter. Heat to boiling, stirring constantly.

Add the water to the flour and mix until smooth. Add slowly to the hot soup, stirring rapidly. Continue to cook, stirring constantly, until the soup is the consistency of heavy cream. Serve hot.

Vegetable Chowder

Yield: 6 to 8 servings

MARGUERITE R. CURTISS, WOMEN OF THE MOOSE (LOYAL ORDER OF MOOSE),
KEENE, NEW HAMPSHIRE

An absolutely terrific chowder made with vegetables and cheese, flavored with tomatoes — a great winter dinner.

2 cups diced and peeled potatoes
1 cup diced celery
1 onion, finely diced (or 1 tablespoon dried onion)
2 teaspoons salt
3 cups water
1/4 cup (1/2 stick) butter or margarine
1/4 cup all-purpose white flour
1 teaspoon dry mustard
3 cups milk
1 tablespoon steak sauce
4 slices American cheese, diced
1 can (28 ounces) tomatoes, chopped
pepper to taste

In a large saucepan or stockpot, combine the potatoes, celery, onion, salt, and water. Cover and bring to a boil; then reduce the heat and simmer until the potatoes are tender, about 15 minutes.

In another saucepan, melt the butter over medium heat. Add the flour and mustard and mix them into the butter to form a paste. Stir in the milk and steak sauce and blend until smooth. Stir in the cheese and continue stirring until the cheese is completely melted. Then add this mixture to the vegetables. Add the tomatoes and pepper and heat through; do not allow the soup to boil. Serve hot.

Baked Fish Chowder

Yield: 4 to 6 servings

ADAPTED FROM A RECIPE BY VERA SHINNER, WOMEN'S ALLIANCE, FIRST PARISH CONGREGATION UNITARIAN CHURCH, KENNEBUNK, MAINE

A quick and easy chowder made in the oven.

1 pound haddock or cod, cut in bite-size pieces
1 pound scallops
3 cups diced peeled potatoes or 8 small unpeeled red potatoes, diced
1 medium-size onion, sliced
1/4 cup white wine
2 cups water
1/4 cup (1/2 stick) butter
1/4 cup all-purpose white flour
2 cups light cream or milk
salt, pepper, and garlic powder to taste

Preheat the oven to 350°F.

In a 9-inch by 13-inch pan, combine the fish, scallops, potatoes, onion, wine, and water. Cover with aluminum foil and bake for 30 minutes.

Melt the butter in a medium-size saucepan over medium heat. Stir in the flour to make a paste. Add the cream or milk and stir until thickened. Add to the baking pan along with the salt, pepper, and garlic powder. Cover and continue baking for another 30 minutes. Stir well before serving.

Seafood Chowder

Yield: 6 to 8 servings

ADAPTED FROM A RECIPE BY NORMA C. GREENE, EMMANUEL CHURCH, NEWPORT, RHODE ISLAND

A very good chowder that fortifies the parishioners for polishing the altar brass.

3 slices bacon
1 onion, chopped
4 to 5 medium-size potatoes, peeled and diced
1 teaspoon salt
water
3/4 pound haddock or other firm white fish or 8 to 10 ounces imitation crab meat, cut in bite-size pieces

(continued)

2 cans (6-1/2 ounces each) tiny shrimp, drained and rinsed
2 cans (6-1/2 ounces each) chopped clams
2 cans (12 ounces each) evaporated milk
1 teaspoon dried basil
1 teaspoon dried thyme
1 tablespoon chopped fresh parsley
salt and pepper to taste

In a large saucepan, fry the bacon. Remove the bacon from the pan, pat dry, crumble, and set aside. Drain off all but 1 tablespoon of the bacon fat. Add the onion and sauté over medium heat until the onion is limp, about 5 minutes. Add the potatoes, salt, and water to cover. Cover and bring to a boil; boil for 5 minutes. Then add the fish and simmer for 5 minutes. Add the remaining ingredients and bring just to a boil. Remove from the heat. Add the crumbled bacon and serve hot.

Peel-A-Pound Soup

Yield: 6 to 8 servings

Ruth Southwick, Willington Baptist Church, Willington, Connecticut

This delicious old-fashioned flavored soup is the perfect way to use up leftover turkey and eat some good-for-you vegetables.

1/2 to 1 pound green cabbage, cut in bite-size pieces
1 green bell pepper, chopped
2 celery stalks, chopped
2 medium-size onions, chopped
1 can (16 ounces) tomatoes, with liquid, chopped
3 bouillon cubes
1 teaspoon celery seeds
1 teaspoon dried basil
2 teaspoons dried oregano
1/2 teaspoon garlic powder
2 or more quarts water
salt and pepper to taste
2 cups diced cooked turkey or beef

Combine all the ingredients in a large saucepan or stockpot, adding enough water to completely cover the vegetables. Bring to a boil, then reduce the heat and simmer for about 1 hour. Serve hot.

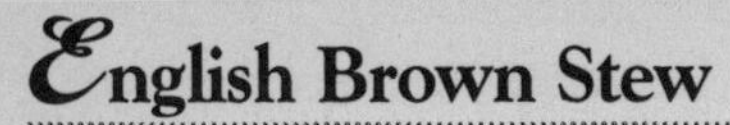

English Brown Stew

***Yield:* 6 to 8 servings**

LUCILE EDWARDS, CHESTER HISTORICAL SOCIETY, CHESTER, NEW HAMPSHIRE

Served with dumplings, muffins, or homemade bread, this delicious cold winter evening meal has a touch of sweetness.

2 pounds London broil, cubed
2 large onions, diced
2 large potatoes, peeled and diced
3 carrots, diced
3 to 4 stalks celery, chopped
2 garlic cloves, minced
1 cup tomato juice or 1 tablespoon tomato paste
1 tablespoon Worcestershire sauce
2 tablespoons lemon juice
2 tablespoons white sugar
1 tablespoon ground allspice
1 tablespoon mild paprika
3 tablespoons beef fat or 2 tablespoons vegetable oil
3 tablespoons all-purpose white flour
salt and pepper to taste

Put the meat in a large saucepan or nonreactive Dutch oven and cover with water. Bring to a boil, then reduce the heat to a simmer, skimming off any foam that rises to the top. When the broth is clear, add the vegetables, tomato juice, Worcestershire sauce, lemon juice, sugar, allspice, paprika, and more water if needed to cover the meat. Simmer until the vegetables are done and the meat is tender, about 2 hours.

In a small saucepan, heat the beef fat or oil. Stir in the flour until you have a smooth paste and cook, stirring constantly, for 1 to 2 minutes. Remove 1/2 to 1 cup of the broth from the stew and stir into the flour mixture until you have a thick gravy. Then pour the gravy into the stew. Add salt and pepper and correct the seasonings. Serve hot.

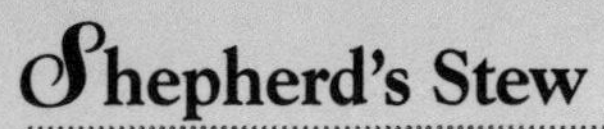

Shepherd's Stew

Yield: 6 servings

PRISCILLA GEER, HANDEL SOCIETY, DARTMOUTH COLLEGE DEPARTMENT OF MUSIC, HANOVER, NEW HAMPSHIRE

Quick and easy to prepare and very good, too.

1 pound sweet or hot Italian sausage, sliced
1 large onion, chopped
6 potatoes, peeled and diced
1 cup sliced celery, including leaves
2 cans (16 ounces each) whole tomatoes
1/4 cup chopped fresh parsley
1-1/2 cups beef broth or stock (or 2 beef bouillon cubes dissolved in 1-1/3 cups water)
1 bay leaf
1/2 teaspoon dried thyme
1/4 teaspoon pepper
juice of 1/2 lemon *(optional)*
salt to taste

In a large saucepan or nonreactive Dutch oven, brown the sausage over medium heat. Add the onion and sauté until transparent, about 5 minutes. Add the remaining ingredients and bring to a boil. Reduce the heat and simmer, uncovered, for 45 to 60 minutes, or until the potatoes are tender. Remove the bay leaf before serving. Serve hot.

Salads & Dressings

Mary's Spinach Salad

Yield: 4 to 6 servings

Mary Gagnon, St. Isaac Jogues Church, East Hartford, Connecticut

A familiar spinach salad with a delightful twist!

Salad:

1 pound spinach
1/2 onion, thinly sliced
1 carrot, grated
2 hard-boiled eggs, quartered
5 slices bacon, fried crisp and crumbled
1 to 1-1/2 cups croutons

Dressing:

1/2 cup honey
1/4 cup water
1/4 cup cider vinegar
1/4 cup ketchup
2 tablespoons minced onion
1 teaspoon Worcestershire sauce

Wash the spinach and drain well. Tear into bite-size pieces. Combine with remaining salad ingredients. Combine the dressing ingredients in a jar and shake well. Just before serving, pour the dressing over the salad and toss to mix.

Seven-Layer Salad

Yield: 10 to 12 servings

Ruth L. Walker, Friends of the Dover Public Library, Dover, New Hampshire

This attractive salad must be made about 8 hours before serving, which makes it convenient for church suppers and potlucks when you don't have time for a lot of last-minute preparations.

1 head lettuce, torn in bite-size pieces
1 cup diced green bell pepper
1 cup chopped celery
1 cup diced onion

(continued)

1 package (10 ounces) frozen peas, thawed
2 cups mayonnaise *(low-fat mayonnaise can be used)*
1 tablespoon white sugar
6 slices bacon, fried crisp and crumbled
3/4 cup grated Cheddar cheese

Place the lettuce in the bottom of a clear salad bowl. On top of the lettuce, layer the pepper, celery, onion and peas in that order. Spoon the mayonnaise over the top to cover and seal the vegetables. Sprinkle the sugar, bacon, and cheese on top. Cover tightly with plastic wrap and refrigerate for 8 hours before serving.

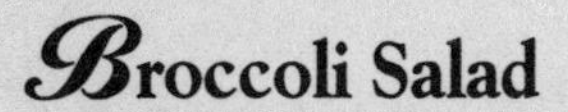

Broccoli Salad

Yield: 6 to 8 servings

GLADYS ANDERSON, WILLINGTON BAPTIST CHURCH, WILLINGTON, CONNECTICUT

Here's a delicious alternative to spinach salad! It incorporates the same flavors as the standard spinach salad, but can be made up to a day in advance and won't wilt on the buffet table.

4 cups broccoli florets
4 hard-boiled eggs, thinly sliced
1/2 cup (or more) thinly sliced onion
10 slices bacon, fried crisp and crumbled
1 cup mayonnaise
1/4 cup white sugar
3 tablespoons vinegar

Blanch the broccoli in boiling water to cover for 30 seconds. Remove the broccoli from the water and plunge it into ice water to stop the cooking. Drain well.

In a large bowl, combine the broccoli, eggs, onion, and bacon. In a small bowl, mix together the mayonnaise, sugar, and vinegar, whisking until the sugar is dissolved. Pour over the broccoli and mix gently. Refrigerate for 6 hours or overnight before serving. Just before serving, toss lightly.

Marinated Vegetables

Yield: 8 to 12 servings

ADAPTED FROM A RECIPE BY BARBARA LITTLE, GOOD SHEPHERD LUTHERAN CHURCH, RUTLAND, VERMONT

A colorful dish that's easy to prepare and is a good, make-ahead recipe that keeps for several days in the refrigerator.

1/2 head cauliflower, in small pieces
2 cups bite-size broccoli florets and stems
2 carrots, sliced
2 celery stalks, sliced 1 inch thick
1 small onion, sliced
1 green bell pepper, cubed
3/4 to 1 cup stuffed green olives or pitted black olives, drained
3/4 cup white or wine vinegar
1/2 cup salad oil
2 tablespoons white sugar
1 teaspoon salt
1/2 teaspoon pepper
1/2 to 1 teaspoon dried oregano or mixed salad herbs
1/4 cup water

Bring a large pot of water to a boil. Add the cauliflower and broccoli and blanch for 1 minute. Drain, then immediately plunge into cold water to stop the cooking. Drain well.

In a large salad bowl, combine all the vegetables with the olives. In a small bowl or jar, mix together the vinegar, oil, sugar, salt, pepper, herbs, and water. Mix well. Pour over the vegetables. Cover the bowl and refrigerate for 8 to 24 hours before serving.

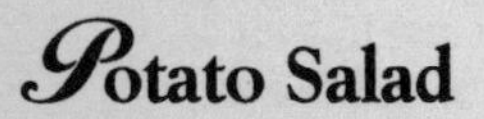

Potato Salad

Yield: 12 to 14 servings

MAUDE R. LARSEN, WALPOLE HISTORICAL SOCIETY, WALPOLE, NEW HAMPSHIRE

An excellent treatment of an old favorite.

8 cups cubed cooked potatoes
1-1/2 cups chopped celery
6 hard-boiled eggs, chopped
2/3 cup chopped radishes
1/2 cup chopped scallions

(continued)

1 cup chopped green bell pepper
1 teaspoon salt
dash pepper
1-1/3 cups Miracle Whip salad dressing
2 tablespoons prepared mustard
Cherry tomato halves, to garnish

In a large bowl, combine the potatoes, celery, eggs, radishes, scallions, green pepper, salt, and pepper. Combine the salad dressing and mustard and add to the potato mixture. Mix lightly. Chill before serving. Garnish with cherry tomato halves.

Hot German Potato Salad

Yield: 15 servings

JANET D. JOHNSON, THE CHURCH OF THE GOOD SHEPHERD, ACTON, MASSACHUSETTS

For those who prefer their potato salad warm!

20 medium-size potatoes
3/4 pound bacon (21 slices)
3/4 cup wine vinegar
1 tablespoon salt
1/2 teaspoon pepper
2 cups thinly sliced scallions

In a heavy pot, cover the potatoes with water. Bring to a boil and cook until the potatoes are tender, about 40 minutes. Drain the potatoes. When cool enough to handle, peel and cut into 1/2-inch cubes. Return the potatoes to the pot.

Fry the bacon until crisp. Remove from the pan, reserving the bacon grease. Drain the bacon, then crumble. To the bacon grease in the pan, add the vinegar, salt, and pepper. Heat over medium heat until bubbling. Remove from the heat.

Pour the dressing over the potatoes. Reserve some scallions and bacon for a garnish and add the remainder to the potatoes. Toss lightly to mix. Cover and let stand for 45 minutes to absorb the seasoning.

Just before serving, set the pot over moderate heat and heat for about 10 minutes. Turn out into a serving bowl. Top with the reserved bacon and scallions and serve.

Italian-Style Pasta Salad

Yield: 4 to 6 servings

Christine Burritt, Henniker Congregational Church, Henniker, New Hampshire

A refreshingly different pasta salad made with vermicelli instead of the usual shells or twist.

4 ounces vermicelli or spaghetti
1 jar (6 ounces) marinated artichoke hearts
1 very small zucchini, halved and thinly sliced
1 carrot, shredded
1/4 pound thinly sliced and chopped cooked ham
1 cup shredded mozzarella
2 tablespoons grated Parmesan cheese
2 tablespoons salad oil
2 tablespoons white wine vinegar
3/4 teaspoon dry mustard
1/2 teaspoon dried oregano
1/2 teaspoon dried basil
1 garlic clove, minced

Cook the pasta according to the package directions and drain well. Drain the artichokes, reserving the marinade. Coarsely chop the artichokes.

In a large bowl, combine the pasta, vegetables, ham, and cheese. In a small bowl or jar, combine the reserved marinade with the oil, vinegar, mustard, and herbs. Mix well. Pour the dressing over the pasta and toss to mix. Chill for several hours.

Chicken Salad

Yield: 12 servings

Adapted from a recipe by Martha McDonald, Harwinton Library Friends, Harwinton, Connecticut

This tasty combination of flavors makes a delicious salad.

6 cups diced cooked chicken
3/4 cup crumbled Roquefort or blue cheese
1/2 cup coarsely chopped walnuts
3/4 cup olive oil
1/3 cup red wine vinegar
1 garlic clove, minced
1/2 cup chopped shallots or scallions

(continued)

1/2 teaspoon salt
1/4 teaspoon pepper
10 cups torn romaine lettuce (bite-size pieces)
4 avocados, sliced, to garnish
1 large red onion, sliced, to garnish
4 oranges, sliced, to garnish

Combine the chicken, cheese, and walnuts in a bowl. In a smaller bowl, combine the oil, vinegar, garlic, shallots, salt, and pepper. Whisk until well combined. Pour over the chicken and toss to mix. Arrange the lettuce on a platter. Mound the salad on top. Garnish with the avocados, red onion, and oranges.

Quick and Easy Salad Dressing

Yield: 1-1/3 cup

GLADYS ANDERSON, WILLINGTON BAPTIST CHURCH, WILLINGTON, CONNECTICUT

A good, simple dressing for a tossed salad or coleslaw. For extra zip on a tossed salad, try using a flavored vinegar, such as tarragon.

1 cup salad oil
1/2 cup vinegar
1/2 cup white sugar
dash salt
1/2 teaspoon celery seeds
1/4 teaspoon garlic salt

Mix all the ingredients together. Shake well before using.

Vegetarian Main Dishes

Baked Ziti

Yield: 6 to 10 servings

ADAPTED FROM A RECIPE BY CLARA E. CARSEN, EMMANUEL CHURCH, NEWPORT, RHODE ISLAND

Enjoy this as a main dish or a side dish. Either way, we guarantee it will not leave you with leftovers. Wonderful dish to take to a potluck!

16 ounces dried ziti
1/2 pound carrots, sliced
1 red or green bell pepper, julienned
1 onion, sliced
1 zucchini, sliced
2 cups grated Cheddar or Swiss cheese
1/4 cup (1/2 stick) butter
1/4 cup all-purpose white flour
3 cups milk
salt and pepper to taste

Preheat the oven to 350°F. Butter a 9-inch by 13-inch baking dish.

Bring a large pot of water to a boil. Cook the ziti and carrots together for about 6 minutes. Drain well. Pour into the baking dish along with the pepper, onion, zucchini, and 1 cup of the cheese.

In a medium-size saucepan, melt the butter. Add the flour and whisk until you have a smooth paste. Slowly add the milk, whisking constantly. Turn the heat to low and cook for 12 to 15 minutes, whisking occasionally. Season to taste with salt and pepper.

Pour the sauce over the pasta and vegetables. Sprinkle the remaining cheese on top. Bake for 30 minutes or until bubbly.

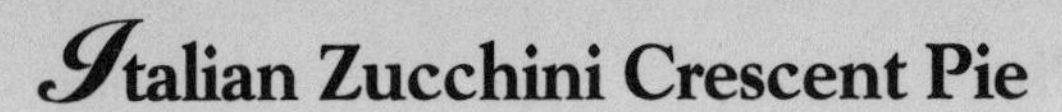

Italian Zucchini Crescent Pie

Yield: 6 to 8 servings

MARILYN D. SERUS, ST. PETER'S EPISCOPAL CHURCH, OXFORD, CONNECTICUT

An easy, delicious and highly recommended recipe.

3 tablespoons margarine or butter
4 cups thinly sliced zucchini
1 cup chopped onion
1/2 cup chopped fresh parsley or 2 tablespoons dried
1/2 teaspoon salt
1/2 teaspoon pepper
1/4 teaspoon garlic powder
1/4 teaspoon dried basil
1/4 teaspoon dried oregano
2 eggs, beaten
8 ounces mozzarella cheese, shredded (2 cups)
1 can (8 ounces) crescent dinner rolls
2 teaspoons prepared mustard

Preheat the oven to 375°F. In a large skillet, melt the margarine over medium heat. Add the zucchini and onion and sauté until the onion is golden, about 10 minutes. Remove from the heat. Stir in the parsley, salt, pepper, garlic powder, basil, and oregano. Combine the eggs and mozzarella and stir into the zucchini mixture.

Place the crescent rolls in an ungreased 10-inch pie plate. Press over the bottom and up the sides to form a crust. Spread the crust with the mustard. Pour the vegetable mixture into the crust. Bake for 18 to 20 minutes or until the center is set. If the crust begins to brown before the center is set, cover with aluminum foil. Let stand for 10 minutes before serving.

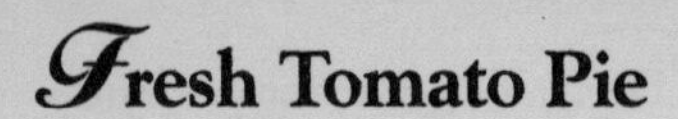

Fresh Tomato Pie

Yield: 4 servings

Shirley Dunlap, Hopkinton Congregational Church, Hopkinton, New Hampshire

Incredibly easy to make, and tastes wonderful!

2 cups Bisquick mix
3/4 cup milk
4 medium-size tomatoes, sliced 1/4 inch thick
1 green bell pepper, sliced
1 teaspoon dried basil
1 teaspoon dried chives
1 teaspoon dried parsley
1-1/2 cups grated sharp Cheddar cheese
1/2 cup mayonnaise

Preheat the oven to 400°F.

Mix together the Bisquick and milk. Press into the bottom and up the sides of a greased 9-inch pie plate. Layer the tomatoes and green pepper in the pie plate, sprinkling each layer with the herbs. Combine the cheese and mayonnaise and spread on top. Bake for 20 to 35 minutes, until the crust and top are golden. Let stand for 10 minutes before serving.

Broccoli Quiche

Yield: 6 servings

Kimberly Ereminas, Harwinton Library Friends, Harwinton, Connecticut

Serve with toasted French bread and slices of fresh tomatoes — delicious!

1 package (10 ounces) frozen chopped broccoli
3 eggs
3/4 cup light cream or milk
1/8 teaspoon salt
1-1/2 cups shredded Monterey Jack cheese
1 can (8 ounces) sliced mushrooms, drained *(optional)*
1 unbaked 9-inch pie shell
paprika

Preheat the oven to 350°F.

Cook the broccoli according to the package directions. Drain the broccoli, plunge it into cold water to stop the cooking, and drain well.

(continued)

In a mixing bowl, beat the eggs, cream, and salt. Stir in the broccoli, cheese, and mushrooms, if using. Pour into the pie shell. Sprinkle with paprika.

Bake for 50 to 60 minutes or until a knife inserted near the center comes out clean. Let stand for 10 minutes before serving.

Vegetable-Cheese Bake

Yield: 6 to 8 servings

BARBARA ECKE, ST. THOMAS BECKET CHURCH, CHESHIRE, CONNECTICUT

The textures of the vegetables are terrific, and the herb stuffing mix adds a nice flavor.

2 tablespoons vegetable oil
1 large onion, chopped
1 large green bell pepper, cubed
1 medium-size eggplant, cubed
8 ounces mushrooms, sliced
1 large tomato, chopped
1 teaspoon salt
3/4 teaspoon dried thyme
1/8 teaspoon pepper
1 cup herb stuffing mix
12 ounces Swiss cheese, shredded

Preheat the oven to 350°F. Butter a 2-quart casserole dish.

Heat the oil in a large skillet over medium heat. Add the onion and green pepper and sauté for 3 minutes. Add the eggplant and mushrooms and sauté for 3 more minutes. Add the tomato and seasonings and cook for 1 minute.

Spread the stuffing mix in the bottom of the casserole. Layer half of the vegetable mixture over the stuffing. Sprinkle with 1 cup of the shredded cheese. Cover with the remaining vegetables. Bake, uncovered, for 30 minutes. Sprinkle with the remaining cheese and bake for 10 more minutes or until the cheese melts.

Main Dishes with Fish & Shellfish

Vermicelli with White Clam Sauce

Yield: 4 to 6 servings

ADAPTED FROM A RECIPE BY REVEREND DAVID M. BLANCHARD, NORTH PARISH CHURCH OF NORTH ANDOVER, UNITARIAN UNIVERSALIST, NORTH ANDOVER, MASSACHUSETTS

White clam sauce can be made with canned clams or fresh littleneck clams, depending on what is available to you. Either way, this pasta dish makes a great quick supper, served with crusty hot bread and a salad on the side.

2 cans (6-1/2 ounces each) minced clams or
1 cup freshly steamed and shucked clams
1/4 cup olive oil
1 to 2 tablespoons butter
4 garlic cloves, crushed
2 to 3 tablespoons chopped fresh parsley
1/2 teaspoon salt
16 ounces dried vermicelli

Drain the clams and reserve the juice. Or measure out 1 cup of the clam-steaming liquid and set aside.

In a medium-size saucepan, heat the olive oil and butter over low heat. Add the garlic and simmer for about 3 minutes, just until the garlic begins to color; do not let the garlic turn brown or the sauce will taste bitter. Add the parsley, salt, and clam juice. Simmer for 10 minutes. Add the clams and cook just enough to heat through.

Meanwhile, cook the pasta in plenty of boiling salted water according to the package directions. Drain. Place the pasta in individual serving bowls and pour the sauce on top.

Salmon with Butter Sauce

Yield: 4 servings

MARY GAGNON, ST. ISAAC JOGUES CHURCH, EAST HARTFORD, CONNECTICUT

A sophisticated dish that you are just as likely to encounter in a restaurant as at your next potluck.

Butter Sauce:

2 large shallots, minced
1/2 cup dry white wine
2 tablespoons crème fraîche
1/2 cup (1 stick) cold unsalted butter, cut into pieces
salt and pepper to taste

Fish:

1-1/2 pounds center-cut salmon fillets with skin
1/2 teaspoon dried thyme
salt and pepper
2 tablespoons unsalted butter
fresh parsley sprigs, to garnish

To make the sauce, combine the shallots and wine in a small saucepan. Bring to a boil and simmer until the wine has almost completely evaporated. Stir in the crème fraîche. Bring the mixture to a boil, stirring constantly. Whisk in the butter, 1 piece at a time, lifting the pan from the heat occasionally to cool the mixture and adding each new piece of butter before the previous one has completely melted. (The sauce should not become hot enough to liquefy.) Add salt and pepper to taste. Keep the sauce warm in the top of a double boiler while you prepare the fish.

To cook the fish, sprinkle the fillets with the thyme, salt, and pepper. Melt the butter in a large heavy skillet. When the foam subsides, add the fish, skin side up, and cook for 2 minutes. Then turn and cook the other side for about 1 minute. Serve with the butter sauce and garnish with parsley.

Note: to make crème fraîche, combine 1 cup whipping cream with 1 teaspoon cultured buttermilk. Heat to 85°F. Cover and let stand at room temperature for 8 to 24 hours, until thickened. Store in the refrigerator.

Quick and Easy Salmon Patties

Yield: 4 to 6 servings

Adapted from a recipe by Frances L. Calder, Chebeague Parents Association, Chebeague Island, Maine

A good recipe for a cold winter night, and the perfect last-minute supper when you don't have time to shop.

1 can (14-3/4 ounces) salmon, bones and skin removed
1 egg
1/3 cup minced onion
1/2 cup all-purpose white flour
1-1/2 teaspoons baking powder
1/2 cup finely crushed crackers or dry bread crumbs
Crisco or canola oil for frying

Drain the salmon, setting aside 2 tablespoons of the liquid. In a medium-size mixing bowl, combine the salmon and 2 tablespoons liquid, the egg, onion, flour, and baking powder. Mix well. Form into small patties and coat the patties with the crushed crackers.

Heat the oil in a large heavy skillet. Fry the patties until golden brown on both sides, about 3 minutes per side. Drain well and keep warm while frying the remaining patties. Serve warm.

Scallops in Wine Sauce

Yield: 4 servings

Gerald T. Littlefield, Chebeague Parents Association, Chebeague Island, Maine

Easy to make and absolutely wonderful!

1/2 cup water
1/3 cup dry white wine
1 teaspoon cider vinegar
1 pound bay scallops
2 tablespoons butter or margarine
2 tablespoons all-purpose white flour
1/3 cup mayonnaise
1/4 teaspoon ground thyme
salt and pepper to taste

(continued)

In a medium-size saucepan, bring the water, wine, and vinegar to a boil. Add the scallops and simmer for 5 minutes. Drain and set aside; reserve the cooking liquid.

Wipe out the saucepan and return to the stove. Add the butter and allow it to melt over medium heat. Stir in the flour and cook for about 5 minutes, stirring constantly. Add the reserved cooking liquids and stir until thickened. Stir in the mayonnaise and thyme. Season to taste with salt and pepper. Add the scallops and serve at once or transfer to a double boiler and keep warm.

Marinated Scallops

Yield: 4 servings

Joan Blanchard, North Parish Church of North Andover, Unitarian Universalist, North Andover, Massachusetts

On the expensive side, like any scallop recipe, but very good. While the scallops marinate, prepare a salad and side dishes.

1 pound bay scallops (or substitute sea scallops cut in quarters)
1/3 cup dry vermouth
1 garlic clove, minced
salt and pepper
1/2 cup dry bread crumbs
6 tablespoons (3/4 stick) butter
minced fresh parsley, to garnish
lemon wedges, to garnish

Marinate the scallops in the vermouth, garlic, and salt and pepper for about 30 minutes. Drain and mix with the bread crumbs. Heat the butter in a large heavy skillet over medium heat. Add the scallops and sauté until they are cooked through, 3 to 4 minutes. Place on a warmed serving platter and garnish with the parsley and lemon wedges.

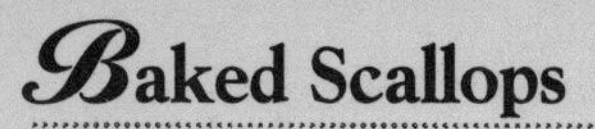

Baked Scallops

Yield: 6 servings

LYNNE MAXIM, ST. ANDREW LUTHERAN CHURCH, ELLSWORTH, MAINE

A great dinner party fare.

2 pounds scallops
1/2 cup (1 stick) butter, melted
1/4 cup grated Parmesan cheese
1 cup crushed Ritz crackers
1 tablespoon lemon juice
1/4 teaspoon pepper
1/4 teaspoon garlic salt
1 tablespoon dry vermouth

Preheat the oven to 325°F. Wash the scallops and pat dry. Place in a buttered 8-inch baking dish. Mix together the remaining ingredients and spoon on top of the scallops. Cover the dish and bake for 30 minutes. Serve hot.

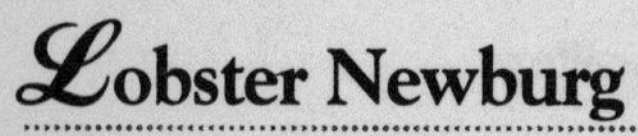

Lobster Newburg

Yield: 4 to 6 servings

BERTHA GRAY, CHEBEAGUE PARENTS ASSOCIATION, CHEBEAGUE ISLAND, MAINE

Coastal New England is known for its wonderful lobster dishes, but this one was actually invented in New York City at the famous Delmonico Restaurant.

2 tablespoons butter
1 tablespoon all-purpose white flour
1-1/3 cups cream (or use part milk)
2 cups (1 pound) cooked lobster meat
3 egg yolks, beaten
1/3 cup sherry
1 teaspoon salt

In the top of a double boiler over simmering water, melt the butter. Add the flour and blend to form a smooth paste. Add the cream and cook until thickened. Add the lobster meat. Stir in the eggs, sherry, and salt. Continue cooking until the sauce has thickened, about 3 minutes. Serve at once, in pastry shells or over rice or toast points.

Shrimp Creole

Yield: 6 servings

ROSEMARY PURDY, ST. THOMAS BECKET CHURCH, CHESHIRE, CONNECTICUT

A dish with southern origins, serve over a bed of fluffy white rice, accompanied by a green salad.

2 tablespoons butter
1 cup chopped onion
1 cup chopped green bell pepper
1 garlic clove, minced
2 cups stewed tomatoes
1/8 teaspoon paprika
salt and pepper to taste
1 pound shrimp, peeled and deveined

In a large heavy skillet, melt the butter over medium heat. Add the onion, green pepper, and garlic and sauté until the pepper is tender, about 5 minutes. Add the tomatoes and seasonings and simmer for 5 minutes. Add the shrimp and simmer for 10 minutes. Serve hot.

Shrimp Casserole

Yield: 8 servings

ADAPTED FROM A RECIPE BY RITA YOUNG, OUR LADY OF GOOD HOPE CATHOLIC WOMEN'S CLUB, CAMDEN, MAINE

A great buffet dish. It should be made well ahead so the flavors have time to meld.

2 pounds cooked, peeled shrimp
6 slices white bread, torn in bite-size pieces
8 ounces cheese (Cheddar is recommended), grated
2 tablespoons butter, melted
3 eggs, lightly beaten
2 teaspoons dry mustard
2 cups milk

Butter a 2-quart casserole dish and layer with half the shrimp, half the bread, and half the cheese. Repeat for a second layer of each, ending with the cheese. Pour the melted butter over the cheese. Beat together the eggs, mustard, and milk. Pour over the casserole. Cover and refrigerate for a least 3 hours, preferably overnight.

Preheat the oven to 350°F. Bake, covered, for 1 hour. Serve warm.

Main Dishes with Chicken & Turkey

Special Roasted Chicken

Yield: 4 servings

SUSAN GAGNON, HOPKINTON COOKIE EXCHANGE, HOPKINTON, NEW HAMPSHIRE

The garlic, lemon, and rosemary flavorings are subtle but delicious!

3-pound to 4-pound roasting chicken
salt and pepper
1 lemon
5 garlic cloves, sliced in half lengthwise
1 tablespoon fresh or dried rosemary
1 teaspoon paprika

Preheat the oven to 350°F. Wash the chicken and remove any loose fat and the giblet bag. Pat dry and sprinkle with salt and pepper inside and out. Place the chicken in a baking dish, breast side up. Wash the lemon thoroughly. Roll the lemon against a countertop several times to burst the juice sacs, making the lemon juicier. With a trussing needle or toothpick, poke 30 to 40 holes in the lemon. Place the lemon inside the chicken cavity. Close the opening of the chicken with toothpicks or a trussing needle. With a sharp knife, make an incision into the chicken breast with a garlic piece resting on the knife's edge. Push the garlic deeper into the chicken meat. Repeat all over the chicken until all the garlic pieces have been inserted. Generously sprinkle the chicken with the rosemary and paprika.

Roast for 20 minutes per pound. Baste once or twice while it roasts. Before serving, remove the lemon carefully; the juices will be hot.

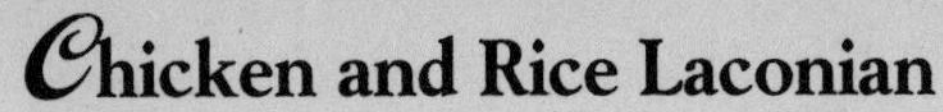

Chicken and Rice Laconian

***Yield:* 4 to 6 servings**

Adapted from a recipe by Diane Speare Triant, The Hellenic Women's Club, EOK of Greater Boston, Wellesley Hills, Massachusetts

A scrumptious Greek recipe brought to America by the contributor's father.

2 to 3 pounds chicken pieces with skins removed (8 to 10 thighs or 5 to 6 breasts)
salt and pepper
2 tablespoons olive oil
1 medium-size onion, cut in thin slivers
2-1/2 cups water
1 tablespoon dried oregano
5 tablespoons ketchup
1 cup uncooked long-grain white rice
1 red bell pepper, cubed
1 cup frozen peas

Wash the chicken and pat dry. Season with salt and pepper and set aside.

In a large, heavy skillet, heat the olive oil over low heat. Add the onion and sauté until limp, about 4 minutes. Add the chicken and cook until brown, about 15 minutes, turning frequently. You will have to do this in a few batches. As the pieces brown, remove them from the skillet and keep them warm. When the last piece is browned, wipe out the skillet with paper towels to remove any excess fat.

Return the chicken to the skillet. Combine the water, oregano, and ketchup and pour over the chicken. Bring to a boil, then simmer, covered, for 1 hour over very low heat (for boneless chicken reduce the cooking time to 30 minutes). Remove the chicken to a platter and cover to keep it warm.

Measure the liquid remaining in the skillet. Add enough water to measure 2 cups. Bring to a boil. Add the rice, stir, and return to a gentle boil. Add the red pepper and peas. Reduce the heat and simmer, covered, for about 14 minutes. Remove from the heat and let stand for 10 minutes. Serve with the chicken.

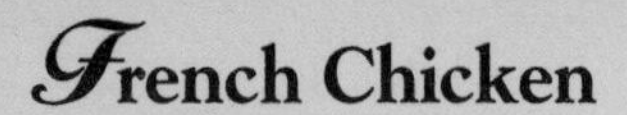

French Chicken

Yield: 4 servings

FLORENCE GRISWOLD MUSEUM, LYME HISTORICAL SOCIETY, OLD LYME, CONNECTICUT

Great flavor for very little effort — serve any extra sauce over rice or buttered noodles for a fabulous meal.

3 tablespoons margarine
3 to 4 pounds chicken quarters
1 small onion, minced
1 teaspoon salt
1/4 teaspoon black pepper
1/4 teaspoon dried thyme
1/4 teaspoon dried basil
3/4 cup dry white wine
2 tablespoons sherry
1 cup light cream
juice of 1/2 lemon

In a large skillet over medium heat, melt the margarine. Add the chicken, onion, salt, and pepper. Cook until the chicken is browned on both sides. Reduce the heat to low, cover and cook for 20 to 30 minutes. Add the thyme, basil, white wine, and sherry and continue cooking for 15 minutes more, or until done.

In a small saucepan, bring the cream to a boil and cook to reduce the volume somewhat. Add the lemon juice.

Transfer the chicken to a serving dish. Add the hot cream to the pan juices and stir briefly over a hot burner. When well blended, pour over the chicken and serve.

Teriyaki-Lemon Chicken

Yield: 6 servings

CARI MARCHESE, NORTH PARISH CHURCH OF NORTH ANDOVER, UNITARIAN UNIVERSALIST, NORTH ANDOVER, MASSACHUSETTS

Crispy on the outside, flavorful on the inside.

3 whole chicken breasts, boned, skinned, and split
1/4 cup all-purpose white flour
2 to 4 tablespoons unsalted butter
1/3 cup teriyaki sauce
3 tablespoons lemon juice
1 teaspoon minced garlic
1/2 teaspoon white sugar

(continued)

Roll the chicken in the flour to coat. Melt the butter in a large heavy skillet over medium heat. Add the chicken and brown on both sides, about 7 minutes per side. Remove the chicken to a plate and keep warm. Add the remaining ingredients to the skillet and mix well. Return the chicken to the skillet and simmer for 3 to 5 minutes. Turn the chicken and simmer for another 3 to 5 minutes, with the pan covered, or until the chicken is cooked through.

Chicken Hawaiian

Yield: 4 servings

ADAPTED FROM A RECIPE BY MYRTLE P. ROWLAND, ST. PETER'S EPISCOPAL CHURCH, OXFORD, CONNECTICUT

A taste of Hawaii in New England. This recipe can be easily extended by adding chunks of onions, mushrooms, bell peppers, carrots, or broccoli. Just steam or sauté the vegetables separately and add to the baking dish during the last 15 minutes of cooking.

2 whole chicken breasts, boned, skinned, and split
1 can (16 or 20 ounces) pineapple chunks in juice
1/4 cup soy sauce
1/2 to 1 teaspoon ground ginger
2 tablespoons cornstarch

Place the chicken, whole or cut into bite-size pieces, in a shallow glass bowl or baking dish. Drain the pineapple. Mix the pineapple juice with the soy sauce and ginger. Pour the mixture over the chicken. Marinate the chicken for 30 to 60 minutes, or overnight in the refrigerator.

Preheat the oven to 400°F. Lightly grease a 9-inch by 13-inch baking dish. Remove the chicken from the marinade, place it in the baking dish, and sprinkle with the cornstarch. Bake for 20 to 25 minutes. Turn the chicken, cover with the pineapple chunks and remaining marinade, and bake for 15 minutes. Serve hot

Savory Buttermilk Chicken

Yield: 6 to 8 servings

Lee Ann Robinson, Chebeague Parents Association, Chebeague Island, Maine

Meltingly tender chicken morsels with a crispy coating flavored with Parmesan cheese.

1-1/2 cups all-purpose white flour
2/3 cup grated Parmesan cheese
3/4 teaspoon paprika
3/4 teaspoon dried oregano
1/4 teaspoon pepper
4 whole chicken breasts, skinned and split
1 cup buttermilk
1/4 to 1/2 cup (1/2 to 1 stick) butter, melted

Preheat the oven to 350°F. Line a baking pan with aluminum foil for easy cleanup.

Mix the flour, cheese, and seasonings in a plastic bag. Dip the chicken in the buttermilk, then in the flour mixture. Arrange in a single layer in the baking pan. Drizzle the melted butter over the chicken. Bake for 50 minutes. Increase the oven temperature to 400°F and bake for another 10 minutes to make the crust crispy. Do not turn the chicken while it is baking. Serve hot

Turkey-Almond Casserole

Yield: 6 servings

Rebecca Phipps McGee, Chebeague Parents Association, Chebeague Island, Maine

Delicious and elegant — and makes good use of leftover cooked turkey or chicken.

1/4 cup (1/2 stick) butter
1/4 cup all-purpose white flour
1 cup chicken broth
3/4 cup milk
2 tablespoons sherry
1/2 teaspoon salt
1/4 teaspoon pepper
4 cups cubed cooked turkey or chicken
1 can (4 ounces) sliced mushrooms, drained
1 can (8 ounces) sliced water chestnuts, drained

(continued)

2/3 cup slivered or whole almonds
1 medium-size onion, minced
paprika

Preheat the oven to 350°F. In a medium-size saucepan, melt the butter over low heat. Blend in the flour. Cook until smooth and bubbly, stirring constantly. Stir in the broth and milk. Heat to boiling, reduce the heat, and simmer until thick. Remove from the heat and stir in the sherry, salt, and pepper.

In a 2-quart baking dish, spread half the turkey. Top with the mushrooms, water chestnuts, almonds, and onion. Arrange the remaining turkey on top. Cover with the sauce. Sprinkle with the paprika and bake for about 45 minutes or until heated through

Wild Rice and Turkey Casserole *Yield: 6 to 8 servings*

ADAPTED FROM A RECIPE BY BOBBY HEAD, STOW HISTORICAL SOCIETY, STOW, MASSACHUSETTS

A combination of wild rice, mushrooms, turkey and almonds — a special way to use holiday leftovers.

1 cup wild rice
1/4 cup (1/2 stick) butter
16 ounces mushrooms, sliced
1/2 cup chopped onion
1-1/4 cups heavy cream
3 cups diced cooked turkey
1/2 cup blanched sliced almonds
3 cups chicken broth
salt and pepper to taste

Wash the rice thoroughly. Place in a large saucepan and cover with water. Bring to a boil, then remove from the heat and set aside for 1 hour. Drain.

Preheat the oven to 350°F. Grease a 2-quart casserole dish.

In a large skillet, melt the butter. Add the mushrooms and onion and sauté until browned, about 8 minutes. Add to the rice, along with the remaining ingredients, and mix well. Spoon into the casserole and bake for about 1 hour, until the rice is tender.

Main Dishes with Meat

Party Casserole

Yield:* 6 to 8 *servings

ADAPTED FROM A RECIPE BY SHIRLEY MARTIN, CHURCH OF THE EPIPHANY, SOUTHBURY, CONNECTICUT

A simple, delicious lasagna for cooks who like to get out of the kitchen fast. Dish can be made ahead and refrigerated until you're ready to bake it.

8 ounces medium-wide spinach noodles
1 to 1-1/2 pounds ground beef
1 onion, finely chopped
2 cans (8 ounces each) tomato sauce
1/2 teaspoon dried oregano
1 package (8 ounces) cream cheese, at room temperature
1/4 cup sour cream
1 cup cottage cheese
3 scallions, finely chopped
1 teaspoon salt
dash pepper
1/4 cup grated Parmesan cheese *(optional)*

Cook the noodles according to the package directions. Drain and set aside.

In a nonstick skillet, brown the meat and the onion. Add the tomato sauce and oregano. Taste and adjust the seasonings, if desired.

Combine the cream cheese, sour cream, cottage cheese, scallions, salt, and pepper.

Preheat the oven to 350°F. To assemble the casserole, grease a 9-inch by 13-inch baking dish. Layer half the noodles, all the cream cheese mixture, the remaining noodles, and the meat sauce. Top with the Parmesan cheese, if desired. Bake for 20 to 30 minutes. Serve hot.

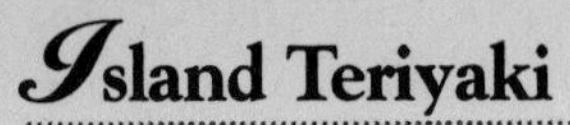

Island Teriyaki

Yield: 4 to 6 servings

RISE CARON, HARWINTON LIBRARY FRIENDS, HARWINTON, CONNECTICUT

Great for a barbecue!

1/2 cup soy sauce
1/4 cup brown sugar
2 tablespoons olive oil
1 teaspoon ground ginger
1/4 teaspoon cracked pepper
2 garlic cloves, minced
1-1/2 pounds beefsteak (sirloin, London broil, etc.)

In a shallow glass baking dish, combine the soy sauce, brown sugar, olive oil, ginger, pepper, and garlic. Add the beef, turning until it is well coated with the marinade. Set aside to marinate for 2 hours at room temperature or longer in the refrigerator. Broil or cook on a grill to desired doneness.

Swedish Meatballs

Yield: 6 to 8 servings

SYLVIA M. BROWN, FIRST UNIVERSALIST CHURCH OF ESSEX, ESSEX, MASSACHUSETTS

An excellent version of an ever-popular buffet dish.

2 slices white bread
3/4 cup milk
1 small onion, finely chopped
2 eggs, lightly beaten
1/4 teaspoon sugar
salt and pepper to taste
2 pounds ground beef
1/2 cup all-purpose white flour
2 tablespoons margarine or vegetable oil

In a mixing bowl, soak the bread in the milk. Add the onion, eggs, sugar, and salt and pepper. Add the ground beef and mix well. Using two spoons or wet hands, form the meat mixture into balls between the size of Ping Pong balls and golf balls. Roll in the flour.

Heat the margarine in a large skillet. Fry the meatballs until golden brown. You will have to fry them in several batches. As the meatballs brown, transfer them to a shallow baking pan and keep warm in a 300°F oven.

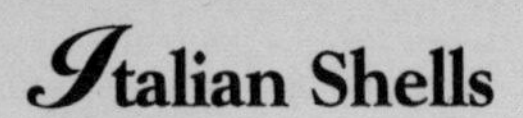

Italian Shells

Yield: 6 to 8 servings

Ellen Moore, St. Brendan's Catholic Woman's Club, Colebrook, New Hampshire

Another do-ahead dish that is popular at a potluck, and can be pulled from the refrigerator and baked just before serving.

1 package (12 ounces) jumbo shells
1 pound ground beef
1 pound hot Italian sausage, casings removed
1 carton (15 ounces) ricotta or low-fat cottage cheese
16 ounces mozzarella cheese, shredded (about 3 cups)
garlic powder, oregano, basil, salt, and pepper to taste
1 jar (14 ounces) spaghetti sauce
grated Parmesan cheese
chopped fresh parsley, to garnish

Cook the shells according to the package directions. Drain, then cover with cold water and set aside.

In a nonstick skillet, brown the meats. Drain off the excess fat. Then add the ricotta and mozzarella and the seasonings to taste.

Preheat the oven to 350°F. Lightly grease a 9-inch by 13-inch baking pan. Remove the shells from the water, fill with the meat-and-cheese mixture, and place in the baking pan. Cover with the sauce. Sprinkle with Parmesan cheese and parsley. Bake for 40 minutes. Serve hot.

Beef 'N' Biscuit Casserole

Yield: 4 to 5 servings

Bill Pahl, Handel Society, Dartmouth College Department of Music, Hanover, New Hampshire

A great supper to rustle up when time is short and the kids are starved.

1 pound ground beef
1/2 cup chopped onion
1/4 cup diced green bell pepper
1 can (8 ounces) tomato sauce
2 teaspoons chili powder
1/2 teaspoon garlic salt
1 can (8 ounces) refrigerator buttermilk biscuits
1-1/2 cups grated Cheddar cheese
1/2 cup sour cream
1 egg, slightly beaten

(continued)

Preheat the oven to 375°F. In a large nonstick skillet, brown the ground beef with the onion and green pepper. Drain off any excess fat. Stir in the tomato sauce, chili powder, and garlic salt. Let simmer.

Separate the biscuit dough into 10 biscuits; split each in half. Press 10 biscuit halves over the bottom of an ungreased 8-inch or 9-inch square baking pan. In a bowl, mix 1/2 cup of the cheese with the sour cream and egg.

Remove the meat mixture from the heat and stir in the sour cream mixture. Spoon over the biscuit dough. Arrange the remaining biscuit halves on top. Sprinkle with the remaining 1 cup of cheese. Bake for 25 to 30 minutes, until golden brown.

Seven-Layer Dinner

***Yield:* 4 to 6 servings**

Carolyn Kelly, Our Lady of Good Hope Catholic Women's Club, Camden, Maine

A perfect one-pot, family-style meal.

1 pound ground beef
4 medium-size potatoes, peeled and sliced
1 cup sliced onions
1/2 cup uncooked rice
1 can (15 ounces) diced tomatoes
1 green bell pepper, sliced
1 stalk celery, sliced
1 cup sliced mushrooms
4 slices bacon
cold water

In a large nonstick skillet, brown the ground beef. Drain off any excess fat. Preheat the oven to 350°F.

Line a 3-quart or 4-quart casserole with the potatoes. Spread the onions over the potatoes, then add the ground beef. Sprinkle the rice over the beef. Pour the tomatoes over all and top with the vegetables. Place the bacon on top of the casserole. Add enough cold water to just cover the casserole. Cover and bake for 1-3/4 hours.

Sweet-and-Sour Meatballs

Yield: 6 to 8 servings

DORIS C. NEUMAN, GOSHEN HISTORICAL SOCIETY, GOSHEN, NEW HAMPSHIRE

Cranberries add a tasty New England touch. Leftovers will keep well in the freezer.

2 pounds lean ground beef
1 cup cornflake crumbs
1/3 cup dried parsley
2 eggs, lightly beaten
2 teaspoons soy sauce
1/4 cup ketchup
2 teaspoons minced onion
2 tablespoons solid vegetable shortening
1 can (16 ounces) whole-berry cranberry sauce
1 bottle (12 ounces) chili sauce
2 teaspoons brown sugar
1 teaspoon lemon juice

Combine the beef with the cornflake crumbs, parsley, eggs, soy sauce, ketchup, and onion and mix well. Using two spoons or wet hands, form the meat mixture into balls between the size of Ping-Pong balls and golf balls.

Preheat the oven to 350°F. Heat the shortening in a large skillet. Fry the meatballs until they are golden brown. You will have to fry them in several batches. As the meatballs brown, transfer them to a shallow baking pan. When the meatballs are browned, make the sauce. Combine the remaining ingredients and pour over the meatballs. Bake for 20 to 30 minutes and serve hot.

Chinese Rice

Yield: 4 to 6 servings

MARIE GOSSELIN, ST BRENDAN'S CATHOLIC WOMAN'S CLUB, COLEBROOK, NEW HAMPSHIRE

A quick, good, and easy recipe that can be made with leftover ham, beef or pork — or with no meat at all.

2 tablespoons vegetable oil
1 cup chopped cooked meat
4 cups cooked white rice (2 cups uncooked)
1/2 cup canned sliced mushrooms, drained
1-1/2 tablespoons chopped scallions

(continued)

1 red bell pepper, diced
2 tomatoes, diced
1 hard-boiled egg, sliced
2 to 3 tablespoons soy sauce (or more to taste)
2 to 3 tablespoons brown sugar
1/4 teaspoon celery seeds

In a large heavy skillet, heat the oil over medium heat. Add the meat and brown slowly. Then add the remaining ingredients and cook for 5 to 7 minutes, stirring often. Serve hot.

Ruth's Lasagna

Yield: 8 to 10 servings

FRED SWALLOW, EAST DOVER BAPTIST CHURCH, EAST DOVER, VERMONT

A good do-ahead dinner. The prepared sauce makes it quicker and easier to fix than most lasagna recipes.

16 ounces dried lasagna noodles
1-1/4 pounds chuck, chopped
1 bottle (26 ounces) spaghetti sauce with mushrooms
1 tablespoon white sugar
1-1/2 pounds cottage cheese
3 eggs, lightly beaten
1/4 teaspoon cayenne pepper
3/4 pound mozzarella cheese, shredded
grated Parmesan cheese
1 cup milk

Cook the lasagna noodles according to the package directions, being sure to add a teaspoon of oil to the cooking water. Rinse and drain.

In a nonstick skillet, brown the meat and drain off any excess fat. Heat the sauce and add the meat to the sauce along with the sugar.

Combine the cottage cheese, eggs, and cayenne.

Preheat the oven to 350°F. To assemble the lasagna, spoon a thin layer of sauce on the bottom of a 9-inch by 13-inch pan. Place a layer of noodles, another thin layer of sauce, a layer of the cottage cheese mixture, then the mozzarella. Repeat until the pan is filled. End with a final layer of sauce and Parmesan cheese. Gently pour milk over the top. Cover with foil and bake for 1 hour. Uncover and let stand for 5 to 10 minutes before cutting into serving-size pieces.

Barbecued Meat Loaves

Yield: 4 servings

Leslie Zimmer, St. Agatha's Church, Milton, Massachusetts

Kids love having their own mini loaves, and the basting helps keep the top from getting too crusty. Serve with mashed potatoes and buttered carrots.

Meat Loaves:

1 pound lean ground beef
1 egg, lightly beaten
1/4 cup fine dry bread crumbs or cornflake crumbs
1 tablespoon dried parsley
1/4 cup water
2 tablespoons chopped onion
2 tablespoons prepared horseradish
1 teaspoon salt
1/8 teaspoon pepper

Sauce:

1/2 cup chili sauce
3 tablespoons ketchup
1 teaspoon Worcestershire sauce
1/2 teaspoon dry mustard
dash Tabasco sauce

Preheat the oven to 350°F. Grease a shallow baking pan.

Combine all the ingredients for the meat loaves. Mix well and shape into four oblong loaves. Place these in the baking pan; do not allow them to touch. Combine the sauce ingredients and spread over the tops and sides of the loaves. Bake for about 45 minutes, basting the loaves two or three times with the drippings that accumulate.

Apple-Glazed Pork Tenderloin

Yield: 6 to 8 servings

Mary Gagnon, St. Isaac Jogues Church, East Hartford, Connecticut

Simple, elegant, with a wonderful flavor.

2 whole pork tenderloins (each about 3/4 pound)
1/2 cup bourbon
1/2 cup unfiltered apple cider
1/4 cup firmly packed brown sugar
1/8 teaspoon cinnamon

(continued)

Place the pork tenderloins in a glass baking dish. Mix the remaining ingredients and pour over the tenderloins. Cover with plastic wrap and refrigerate for 8 hours or more, turning the meat several times. (If you need more marinade, add 1/4 cup more cider.)Preheat the oven to 325°F. Place the baking dish with the meat and marinade in the oven and bake for 1-1/4 hours or until the internal temperature of the meat reaches 160°F (medium well) to 170°F (well-done). While the meat bakes, baste with the marinade every 10 or 15 minutes. Let stand for 10 to 15 minutes before carving.

Shredded Potato and Ham Pie

Yield: 6 servings

CHRISTINE BURRITT, HENNIKER CONGREGATIONAL CHURCH, HENNIKER, NEW HAMPSHIRE

A great brunch or dinner dish that's easily doubled to feed a larger group.

4 eggs, slightly beaten
1 cup frozen mixed peas and carrots
1 cup chopped cooked ham
1-1/2 cups shredded Cheddar cheese (6 ounces)
1/2 cup milk
1/4 teaspoon dried minced onion or 1 tablespoon minced fresh onion
2 medium-size potatoes, peeled and shredded (about 2 cups)

Preheat the oven to 350°F. In a mixing bowl, combine the eggs, peas and carrots, ham, 1 cup of the cheese, the milk, and the onion. Mix well. Set aside.

Combine the shredded potatoes and remaining 1/2 cup cheese. Press the potato mixture onto the bottom and up the sides of an ungreased 9-inch pie plate or 8-inch square baking dish. Pour the filling over the potato mixture. Bake for 45 to 50 minutes or until the center is set. Let stand for 5 minutes before slicing in wedges or squares. Serve warm.

Cranberry Pork Chops

Yield: 4 servings

LAWNIE ROBERGE, STOW HISTORICAL SOCIETY, STOW, MASSACHUSETTS

Very simple and very tasty.

4 thick-cut pork chops
1 can (16 ounces) whole-berry cranberry sauce
1 tablespoon honey
1/4 teaspoon ground cloves
4 orange slices with peel, to garnish (optional)

Preheat the oven to 350°F. In a large skillet, brown the pork chops. Place the chops in a baking dish. Mix together the cranberry sauce, honey, and cloves. Pour over the pork chops. Cover and bake for 1 hour. Garnish with the orange slices.

Hot Peppered Lamb

Yield: 4 servings

CHARLES KUNTZ, CHEBEAGUE PARENTS ASSOCIATION, CHEBEAGUE ISLAND, MAINE

Add leftover lamb to this well-spiced dish and serve with white or brown rice — sure to be a hit.

1/4 cup (1/2 stick) butter
1/3 cup chopped sweet or hot peppers
2 medium-size onions, chopped
1 cup chopped fresh mushrooms
2 garlic cloves, minced
1/2 teaspoon curry powder
1/2 teaspoon salt
black pepper to taste
1-1/2 cups diced cooked lamb

In a large skillet over medium heat, melt the butter. Add the peppers and onions and sauté until limp, about 4 minutes. Add the remaining ingredients and sauté over high heat until the lamb is heated through and the mushrooms are golden, 4 to 5 minutes.

 Meat Pie

Yield: 6 servings

ADAPTED FROM A RECIPE BY LOIS SPRAGUE, OUR LADY OF GOOD HOPE CATHOLIC WOMEN'S CLUB, CAMDEN, MAINE

A winning combination, guaranteed to please.

Filling:

3 tablespoons vegetable oil
1-1/2 pounds lamb, beef, pork, or veal, diced
1 large onion, chopped
2 cups peeled and diced potatoes
2 cups diced turnips
1 cup sliced carrots
1 cup water
1 tablespoon salt (or to taste)
1/8 teaspoon pepper

Crust:

1-1/2 cups all-purpose white flour
1 tablespoon baking powder
1 teaspoon salt
3 tablespoons butter or solid vegetable shortening
3/4 cup milk (can use skim or low-fat)

Preheat the oven to 275°F. Grease an 8-inch square baking dish.

In a large skillet, heat the oil over medium-high heat. Add the meat and onion and cook until the meat is browned. Drain off any excess fat. Place the meat in the baking dish along with the vegetables, water, 1 tablespoon salt, and pepper. Cover and bake for 2-1/2 hours. (This can be done a day or so in advance and the mixture refrigerated.)

About 45 minutes before serving, preheat the oven to 400°F. Combine the flour, baking powder, and salt for the crust in a mixing bowl. Cut in the butter or shortening until the mixture resembles coarse meal. Add the milk and stir to form a dough. Drop by the spoonful on top of the meat and vegetables, leaving a few openings for steam to escape. Bake for about 30 minutes. Serve hot.

Vegetables & Side Dishes

Green Beans Viennese

Yield: 6 servings

Carolyn Marshall, New England Historic Genealogical Society, Boston, Massachusetts

An easy, very good, side dish that can be made ahead, kept refrigerated and then reheated at the last minute in the oven or microwave.

1 package (16 ounces) frozen cut green beans
1 tablespoon butter
1/4 cup chopped onion
1 tablespoon all-purpose white flour
1 teaspoon salt
dash pepper
1/2 cup chicken broth
2 tablespoons snipped fresh parsley
1 tablespoon vinegar
1/4 teaspoon dried dillweed
1/2 cup sour cream

Cook the beans according to the package directions; drain and set aside.

In the same saucepan, melt the butter. Add the onion and sauté over medium heat until limp, about 3 minutes. Stir in the flour, salt, and pepper. Then add the broth, parsley, vinegar, and dill. Cook, stirring constantly, until the sauce is thick and bubbling. Reduce the heat to low and stir in the sour cream. Add the drained beans. Continue to cook until the beans are heated through, but do not boil.

If you want to make this dish in advance, pour the bean mixture into an 8-inch square glass baking dish. Before serving, heat in a microwave on high for about 10 minutes, stirring every few minutes. Or place in a preheated 350°F oven for about 45 minutes, stirring occasionally, until heated through.

Nutty Brussels Sprouts

***Yield:* 6 servings**

SUSAN B. SHIELDS, WOMEN'S ALLIANCE, FIRST PARISH CONGREGATION UNITARIAN CHURCH, KENNEBUNK, MAINE

Ginger and walnuts make a lovely complement to this much-maligned vegetable. Recipe can be easily doubled to feed a small crowd.

2 packages (10 ounces each) frozen brussels sprouts
1/4 cup (1/2 stick) margarine or butter
3/4 cup chopped walnuts
3/4 teaspoon salt
1/2 teaspoon ground ginger

In a large saucepan, bring 1 inch of salted water to a boil. Add the brussels sprouts and cook until tendercrisp, about 5 minutes. Drain well.

Meanwhile, in a large skillet, melt the margarine over medium-low heat. Add the walnuts, salt, and ginger and cook, stirring occasionally, until the nuts are lightly browned. Add the drained brussels sprouts and toss well. Serve hot.

Cinnamon Carrots

***Yield:* 6 servings**

JEANETTE DEJONG, EAST DOVER BAPTIST CHURCH, EAST DOVER, VERMONT

Tasty and incredibly easy. Serve hot in winter or at room temperature on a hot summer day.

1 to 1-1/2 pounds carrots, sliced
1/3 cup butter, at room temperature
1/2 cup white sugar
1 teaspoon salt
1/4 to 1/2 teaspoon ground cinnamon
1/3 cup boiling water

Preheat the oven to 350°F. Place the carrots in a 1-1/2-quart casserole or baking dish.

Cream together the butter, sugar, salt, and cinnamon. Stir in the boiling water. Pour over the carrots. Bake for 1 hour. Or cook on high in a microwave for 10 minutes.

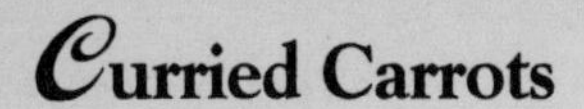

Curried Carrots

***Yield:* 4 to 6 servings**

SUSAN GAGNON, HOPKINTON COOKIE EXCHANGE, HOPKINTON, NEW HAMPSHIRE

A simple but exotic dish that enhances the common carrot.

1 pound carrots, sliced 1 inch thick
2 tablespoons butter
2 to 3 teaspoons curry powder
1/4 teaspoon pepper
1 tablespoon lemon juice
1 tablespoon honey
1/3 cup chopped pecans or walnuts

Place the carrots in a saucepan with water to cover, bring to a boil, and simmer for 15 to 20 minutes or until tender. Drain and return the carrots to the pan. Over low heat, add the remaining ingredients. Mix well and serve immediately.

Scalloped Spinach

***Yield:* 6 to 8 servings**

JEAN JENKINS, CHESTER HISTORICAL SOCIETY, CHESTER, NEW HAMPSHIRE

A traditional favorite at potlucks. You can easily double the recipe for a hungry crowd.

3 package (10 ounces each) frozen chopped spinach
1/2 to 1 package dry onion soup mix
1 cup sour cream
bread crumbs
butter
1/4 cup grated Parmesan cheese

Preheat the oven to 350°F. Cook and drain the spinach. Combine with the soup mix and sour cream. Spoon into a buttered shallow casserole dish. Cover with the bread crumbs, dabs of butter, and the Parmesan cheese. Bake for about 35 minutes. Serve hot.

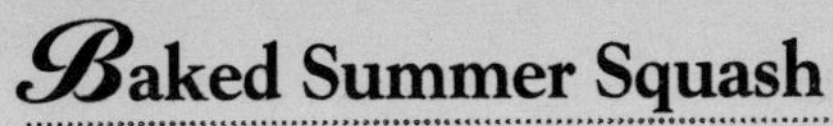

Baked Summer Squash

Yield: 6 servings

ELAINE B. CIARCIA, HARWINTON LIBRARY FRIENDS, HARWINTON, CONNECTICUT

This vegetable dish can be mixed a day ahead and stored in the refrigerator until you're ready to bake it.

3 pounds yellow squash or zucchini
1/2 cup (1 stick) butter, melted
1/2 cup chopped onion
2 eggs, lightly beaten
1 tablespoon sugar
1 teaspoon salt
1/2 teaspoon pepper
1 cup fresh bread crumbs

Slice the squash. Boil or steam until tender. Drain, then mash. Preheat the oven to 375°F.

In a mixing bowl, combine the squash with half the melted butter, the onion, eggs, sugar, salt, and pepper. Spoon into a 2-quart casserole dish. Combine the bread crumbs with the remaining butter and sprinkle over the squash. Bake for about 45 minutes and serve hot.

Maple-Nut Winter Squash

Yield: 8 to 10 servings

ANN P. WHITCOMB, SPRINGFIELD ART AND HISTORICAL SOCIETY, SPRINGFIELD, VERMONT

Very easy and very tasty!

2 large buttercup or medium-size butternut squash
1/3 cup maple sugar or brown sugar
1/3 cup margarine or butter, at room temperature
1/2 to 3/4 cup chopped nuts (walnuts, pecans, or hickory nuts)

Preheat the oven to 350°F. Cut whole squash in half lengthwise and remove the seeds. Place the squash, cut side down, in a baking dish and bake for 30 to 40 minutes, or until tender. Or cut the squash into chunks, remove the seeds, and steam until tender. Scoop the flesh from the skins and mash. Spoon into a casserole dish.

In a small bowl, blend the sugar and margarine. Add the nuts. Spoon on top of the squash. Return to the oven and bake until the squash is hot and the nuts are toasted, 20 to 30 minutes. Serve hot.

Golden Potato Squares

Yield: 8 to 10 servings

CHRISTINE BURRITT, HENNIKER CONGREGATIONAL CHURCH, HENNIKER, NEW HAMPSHIRE

An easy dish that makes potatoes something special!

5 pounds potatoes
2/3 cup butter, melted
1 cup chopped onion
1 can (12 ounces) evaporated milk
4 eggs, beaten
2-1/2 teaspoons salt
1/4 teaspoon pepper
2-1/4 cups shredded Cheddar cheese

Peel the potatoes and place in cold water to prevent discoloration. Set aside. Preheat the oven to 350°F. Grease a 9-inch by 13-inch baking dish.

Melt the butter in a large skillet. Add the onion and sauté until limp, about 5 minutes. Add the milk and bring to a boil. Remove from the heat.

In a large bowl, combine the eggs, salt, and pepper. Beat until frothy. Shred the potatoes and add to the egg mixture. Toss to combine. Add the milk mixture. Set aside 3/4 cup of the cheese, add the rest to the potato mixture, and mix well. Spoon the mixture into the prepared baking dish. Bake for 1 hour. Top with the reserved cheese and bake for an additional 30 minutes. Cut into squares and serve hot.

Orange-Glazed Sweet Potatoes

Yield: 6 servings

MARY GAGNON, ST. ISAAC JOGUES CHURCH, EAST HARTFORD, CONNECTICUT

The sauce recipe can be made a few days ahead, just refrigerate until you're ready to use it.

6 sweet potatoes or 1 can (15 ounces) vacuum-packed sweet potatoes (no syrup)
3 tablespoons butter
1 tablespoon cornstarch
1 cup orange juice
1/3 cup white sugar
1/3 cup light brown sugar
pinch salt

(continued)

If you are using fresh sweet potatoes, cook in boiling salted water for 30 minutes. Peel. Slice the canned or freshly cooked potatoes in half lengthwise. Place in a casserole dish and set aside.

Preheat the oven to 350°F. In a small saucepan, melt the butter. Add the cornstarch and stir until dissolved and smooth. Add the orange juice, stirring constantly. Then add the sugars and salt. Cook over medium heat, stirring constantly, until the sauce is thickened.

Pour the sauce over the sweet potatoes. Bake for 30 minutes. Serve hot.

Zucchini Provençal

Yield: 6 to 8 servings

GLORIA A. OGIELA, MARK TWAIN LIBRARY, REDDING, CONNECTICUT

A new, delicious way to serve zucchini.

3 tablespoons olive oil
2/3 cup chopped onion
4 ounces mushrooms, sliced
8 to 10 small zucchini (2-1/2 pounds), sliced 1/4 inch thick
2/3 cup grated Parmesan cheese (3 ounces)
2 cans (6 ounces each) tomato paste
1 garlic clove, minced
1 teaspoon salt
1/8 teaspoon pepper

Preheat the oven to 350°F.

Heat the oil in a large saucepan. Add the onion and mushrooms and sauté until the onion is limp, about 3 minutes. Add the zucchini and continue sautéing until the zucchini is just tender, about 4 minutes. Remove from the heat and stir in half the cheese. Add the tomato paste, garlic, salt, and pepper. Mix well. Turn into a 2-quart casserole dish and sprinkle the remaining cheese on top. Bake for 20 minutes or until heated through. Serve hot.

Breads & Muffins

ill Bread

Yield:* 1 *loaf

MARCIA GOODNOW, FRIENDS OF THE DOVER PUBLIC LIBRARY, DOVER, NEW HAMPSHIRE

An unusual, very moist bread.

1 package active dry yeast
1/4 cup warm water
1 cup creamed cottage cheese
2 tablespoons honey
1 tablespoon chopped onion
1 tablespoon butter
3 tablespoons dried dillweed, dill seed, or a combination of both
1 teaspoon baking soda
1 egg, slightly beaten
2-1/2 cups all-purpose white flour
melted butter to glaze

Combine the yeast with the warm water. Set aside.

In a saucepan over low heat, combine the cottage cheese, honey, onion, butter, dill, baking soda, and egg. When the butter is melted, remove from the heat. Stir in the yeast mixture. Gradually add the flour to form a stiff dough. Turn out onto a lightly floured board and knead for 5 to 10 minutes.

Place in a large, well-greased bowl and let rise until doubled in bulk, about 1 hour. Punch down, shape into a loaf, and place in a greased 8-inch by 4-inch loaf pan. Let rise until doubled again, about 40 minutes. Preheat the oven to 350°F. Bake for 40 to 50 minutes. Brush the top with butter while the bread is still warm.

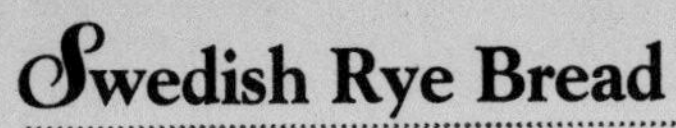

Swedish Rye Bread

Yield: 3 loaves

RUTH CARLSON, GUSTAF ADOLPH LUTHERAN CHURCH, NEW SWEDEN, MAINE

If three loaves are more than you can use, just halve the recipe and make one large and one small loaf.

2 packages active dry yeast
4 tablespoons white sugar
1/2 cup warm water
2 cups hot water
1 cup cold water
1 cup milk
3 cups rye flour
9 to 10 cups all-purpose white flour
1 tablespoon salt
1/2 cup solid vegetable shortening, melted
1 cup (overflowing) molasses
melted butter or margarine to glaze

In a small bowl, combine the yeast with 2 tablespoons of the sugar and 1/2 cup warm water. Mix until foamy.

In a very large bowl, combine the hot and cold water with the milk. Let cool. Add the yeast mixture and stir well. Sift the rye flour, 3 cups of the white flour, the salt, and the remaining 2 tablespoons of sugar into the bowl. Stir well. Add the shortening and molasses and stir. Stir in 4 cups or more of the white flour. Turn out onto a floured board and knead. Keep working in more flour; knead for 5 minutes or more until a good solid ball is formed.

Grease your hands, then place the ball of dough into a greased bowl. Cover. Let rise for 1-1/2 hours and punch down. Let rise for another 1-1/2 hours and punch down again.

Divide the dough into thirds. Put into three well-greased 8-inch by 4-inch loaf pans and let rise for another hour. Preheat the oven to 375°F. Bake for 50 minutes. Brush on melted butter or margarine while the loaves are still warm. Cool for 10 minutes on wire racks, then turn out of the pans to cool completely.

Super Bran Bread

Yield: 2 loaves

Yvonne Menzone, Auburn Group of Worcester County Extension Service, Auburn, Massachusetts

A perfect substitute for brown bread — goes especially well with baked beans.

2 cups All-bran cereal
1/3 cup solid vegetable shortening
1 cup molasses
1-1/2 cups boiling water
2 eggs
2 cups bread flour
2 teaspoons baking soda
1/2 teaspoon salt
1 teaspoon ground cinnamon

Preheat the oven to 350°F. Grease two 8-inch by 4-inch loaf pans.

In a large mixing bowl, combine the cereal, shortening, and molasses. Add the boiling water and stir until the shortening is melted. Add the eggs and beat well. Add the remaining ingredients and mix thoroughly. Pour into the prepared pans.

Bake for 35 to 40 minutes or until a tester inserted near the center of the loaves comes out clean. Cool in the pans for 10 minutes before turning out onto wire racks to finish cooling.

Double Corn Bread

Yield: 9 servings

Mildred K. Ladd, Brentwood Historical Society, Brentwood, New Hampshire

A quick, easy, and inexpensive traditional New England corn bread.

1 cup all-purpose white flour
1 cup yellow cornmeal
4 teaspoons baking powder
1/2 teaspoon salt
4 tablespoons white sugar (or more or less to taste)
1 can (11 ounces) corn
approximately 3/4 cup milk
1 egg, slightly beaten
1/4 cup (1/2 stick) butter or margarine, melted

(continued)

Preheat the oven to 400°F. Grease an 8-inch square baking pan.

In a 1-quart bowl, combine the flour, cornmeal, baking powder, salt, and sugar. Drain the corn, pouring the liquid into a glass measure. Fill the glass measure with milk to make 1 cup. Add to the cornmeal mixture along with the corn kernels, egg, and melted butter. Stir just enough to moisten the dry ingredients. The batter will be lumpy. Spoon into the prepared baking dish.

Bake for 20 to 25 minutes or until a tester inserted near the center comes out clean. Serve warm or cooled.

Strawberry Bread

Yield: 3 loaves

Phyllis Curtis, Church of the Epiphany, Southbury, Connecticut

Perfect for holiday gift giving.

1 cup (2 sticks) butter, at room temperature
1-1/2 cups white sugar
1 teaspoon vanilla extract
1/4 teaspoon lemon extract
4 eggs
3 cups all-purpose white flour
1 teaspoon salt
1/2 teaspoon baking soda
1 teaspoon cream of tartar
1 cup strawberry preserves
1/2 cup sour cream
1 cup chopped nuts

Preheat the oven to 350°F. Grease three 8-inch by 4-inch loaf pans.

In a mixing bowl, cream the butter, sugar, vanilla, and lemon extract until soft. Add the eggs one at a time, beating well after each addition. In another bowl, sift together the flour, salt, soda, and cream of tartar. In a third bowl, combine the preserves, sour cream, and nuts. Add the preserves mixture alternately with the dry ingredients to the creamed mixture. Spoon into the loaf pans.

Bake for 50 minutes or until a tester inserted in the loaves comes out clean. Cool on racks for 10 minutes before removing from the pans to cool completely.

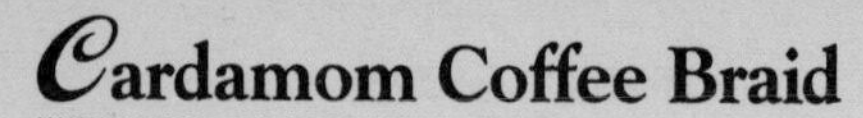

Cardamom Coffee Braid

***Yield:** 16 servings*

BARBARA ANDERSON, ST. PAUL LUTHERAN CHURCH, EAST LONGMEADOW, MASSACHUSETTS

A traditional Scandinavian yeast bread.

Bread:

1-1/2 cups milk
1 package active dry yeast or 1 cake yeast
3/4 cup white sugar
6-1/4 cups sifted all-purpose white flour
1/2 cup (1 stick) butter or margarine, at room temperature
2 egg yolks and 1 whole egg
1 teaspoon ground cardamom
1/4 teaspoon salt

Topping:

2 tablespoons milk
6 tablespoons white sugar

Scald the 1-1/2 cups milk and cool to lukewarm. Crumble the yeast into a bowl and add 1 tablespoon of the sugar and the lukewarm milk. Beat in 3 cups of the flour with an electric mixer, beating until smooth. Cover and let rise until light and doubled in bulk, 1 to 1-1/2 hours.

Add the butter, remaining sugar, egg yolks and egg, cardamom, and salt and mix in. Gradually add 3 cups flour. Pour 1/4 cup flour on a board, turn out the dough, and knead until smooth and elastic. Use only as much more flour as needed to keep the bread from sticking.

Place the dough in a greased bowl. Cover and let rise until doubled in bulk, 1 to 1-1/2 hours.

Cut risen dough in half for 2 braids. Cut each half into 3 pieces. Roll each piece into a rope 16 inches long. Pinch the 3 ropes together at one end. Braid ropes and pinch other ends together. Place on a greased baking sheet. Make second braid and place on second baking sheet.

Let braids rise until doubled in bulk, about 45 minutes. Preheat the oven to 350°F. Before placing breads in oven, brush each with 1 tablespoon milk and sprinkle with 3 tablespoons sugar. Bake for 30 minutes, until golden brown.

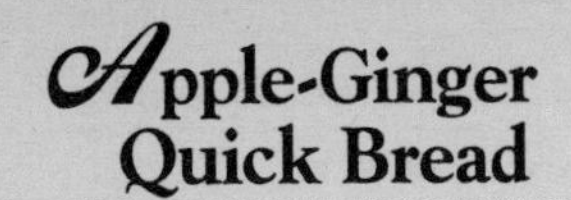

Apple-Ginger Quick Bread

Yield: 1 loaf or 6 mini bundt cakes

ADAPTED FROM A RECIPE BY CECILIA BENNETT, THEODORE PARKER UNITARIAN UNIVERSALIST CHURCH, WEST ROXBURY, MASSACHUSETTS

For gifts, or a pleasant change of pace, bake in mini bundt pans. This bread freezes well, too.

2 cups whole-wheat pastry flour or all-purpose white flour
2 teaspoons baking powder
2 teaspoons ground ginger
1 teaspoon salt
2 large eggs, beaten
1/2 cup brown sugar
1/2 cup vegetable oil
3 medium-size tart apples, peeled and cut into 1/2-inch cubes
1/2 cup raisins and/or 1/2 cup unsalted mixed nuts *(optional)*

Preheat the oven to 350°F. Grease an 8-inch by 4-inch loaf pan or 6 mini bundt pans.

Sift together the flour, baking powder, ginger, and salt; set aside. Combine the remaining ingredients and blend thoroughly. Add the liquid ingredients to the dry ingredients and combine just until blended thoroughly (do not beat). Pour into the prepared pan(s).

Bake the loaf pan for 80 minutes, the mini bundt pans for 60 minutes, or until a tester inserted in the loaves comes out clean. Cool on a rack for 10 minutes before removing from the pans.

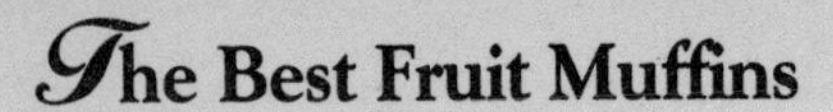

The Best Fruit Muffins

Yield: 12 muffins

CAROLYN MULLER, ST. PETER'S EPISCOPAL CHURCH, WESTON, MASSACHUSETTS

For taste, use regular sour cream, not lowfat or nonfat. The contributor recommends apples, peaches, blueberries, raisins (and nuts), or candied ginger.

1 cup white sugar
1 egg
1 cup sour cream
1/4 cup vegetable oil
1-3/4 cups all-purpose white flour
1 teaspoon baking soda
1/2 teaspoon salt
1 cup diced fruit

Preheat the oven to 400°F. Grease 12 muffin cups.

In a food processor, combine the sugar, egg, sour cream, and oil. Pulse until well blended. In a separate bowl, combine the flour, soda, and salt. Add to the food processor and pulse just to blend. Stir in the fruit. Spoon the mixture into the muffin cups, filling them three-quarters full. Bake for 20 minutes or until a tester inserted in the center comes out clean.

Zucchini-Oatmeal Muffins

Yield: 12 muffins

ADAPTED FROM A RECIPE BY CONNIE MACKAY, ST. ANDREW LUTHERAN CHURCH, ELLSWORTH, MAINE

Nice and crusty on top (even after freezing and reheating in the microwave), moist and delicious on the inside.

2 eggs, beaten
1 medium-size zucchini (about 10 ounces), shredded
1/4 cup vegetable oil
1 cup plain yogurt
2-1/2 cups all-purpose white flour
1 cup white sugar
1/2 cup rolled oats (not instant)
1 tablespoon baking powder

(continued)

1 teaspoon salt
1 teaspoon ground cinnamon
1 cup chopped pecans

Preheat the oven to 400°F. Grease 12 muffin cups or line with paper.

In a large mixing bowl, mix together the eggs, zucchini, oil, and yogurt. Set aside. In another bowl, whisk together the flour, sugar, oats, baking powder, salt, and cinnamon. Add to the zucchini mixture and stir just to moisten. Stir in the pecans. The batter will be lumpy. Spoon into the prepared muffin cups and bake for about 25 minutes or until a tester inserted in the center comes out clean. Do not overbake.

Maple Syrup-Bran Muffins

Yield: 12 muffins

FLORENCE GRISWOLD MUSEUM, LYME HISTORICAL SOCIETY, OLD LYME, CONNECTICUT

These muffins are best served warm from the oven, so a pat of butter can melt in.

1 egg
1/2 cup sour cream
1/2 cup maple syrup
3/4 cup all-purpose white flour
1 teaspoon baking soda
1-1/4 cups branflakes
1/4 cup raisins
1/4 cup chopped pecans

Preheat the oven to 350°F. Grease 12 muffin cups or line with paper.

In a large mixing bowl, beat the egg. Add the sour cream and maple syrup and beat to combine. Set aside. In another bowl, sift the flour with the soda. Add to the egg mixture along with the branflakes and stir just to moisten. The batter will be lumpy. Stir in the raisins and nuts. Spoon into the prepared muffin cups and bake for 20 minutes. Serve hot.

Recipes to Feed a Crowd

Griddle Cakes

***Yield:* 65 servings**

KATHERINE E. PERKINS, THE FEMALE CHARITABLE SOCIETY, FIRST CHURCH OF CHRIST, LANCASTER, MASSACHUSETTS

A time honored recipe from the First Church of Christ.

20 cups sifted all-purpose white flour
3 cups white sugar
6 tablespoons plus 2 teaspoons baking soda
20 eggs
5 quarts buttermilk (or sour milk)
1-1/4 cups (2-1/2 sticks) butter or margarine, melted

In a large bowl, combine the flour, sugar, and soda. Mix with a whisk to blend well.

In a large mixing bowl, beat the eggs. Add the buttermilk and melted butter and blend well. Add the dry ingredients and mix well.

Cook the pancakes on a lightly oiled griddle. Serve hot.

Janie's Bridesmaid Salad

***Yield:* 20 servings**

ELLEN MOORE, ST. BRENDAN'S CATHOLIC WOMAN'S CLUB, COLEBROOK, NEW HAMPSHIRE

An easy-to-prepare dish, sweet enough to be served as a dessert.

2 packages (10 ounces each) frozen strawberries
1 can (14 ounces) sweetened condensed milk
1 container (8 ounces) Cool Whip
1 can (20 ounces) crushed pineapple, with juice
2-1/2 cups (half of a 10-ounce bag) miniature marshmallows, colored variety if available
1/2 cup chopped nuts *(optional)*

(continued)

Partially thaw the berries. Combine in a 12-cup bowl with the condensed milk, Cool Whip, pineapple, and marshmallows. Mix well. Freeze until solid.

Remove from the freezer about 1 hour before serving. Sprinkle with the nuts, if desired.

Cole Slaw

Yield:* 24 *servings

EDITH DOWNING, KILLINGWORTH CONGREGATIONAL CHURCH, KILLINGWORTH, CONNECTICUT

As a general rule, use 1/2 cup dressing for every 2 cups cabbage, and allow 1/2 cup cabbage per person.

4 cups mayonnaise
1 cup sugar
1 cup vinegar
4 teaspoons salt
1/4 teaspoon pepper
8 teaspoons prepared mustard
2 teaspoons celery seed
12 cups shredded cabbage

Blend together all ingredients except cabbage thoroughly with electric mixer or blender. Toss with cabbage and chill.

Corn Chowder

Yield:* 50 *servings

MILDRED A. DIMOCK, ELLINGTON CONGREGATIONAL CHURCH, ELLINGTON, CONNECTICUT

With cold sliced ham (or hot dogs), rolls, and salad, an excellent supper.

1/2 pound salt pork, cut into 1/4" dice
1 pound onions, chopped fine
5 pounds potatoes, peeled and diced
4 to 5 quarts water (to cover potatoes)
2 gallons milk
8 1-pound cans cream-style corn
salt to taste
2 teaspoons pepper
butter

Fry out salt pork, remove browned bits, and reserve. Add onions to fat, and sauté until transparent. Add potatoes and cover with water. Boil gently until potatoes are tender, and pour off cooking water. Add milk, corn, salt pork bits, and seasonings and heat but do NOT boil. Add butter at serving time.

Fruit Bread Pudding

Yield: 25 to 30 servings

EMMA MAZZEO, DAUGHTERS OF ST. BERNARD, ST. BERNARD'S CHURCH, ROCKLAND, MAINE

A rich variation of an old classic.

2 loaves raisin bread
2 cans (12 ounces each) evaporated milk
3 cups whole milk
5 eggs
3 ripe bananas, mashed
1 teaspoon ground cinnamon
1 teaspoon ground nutmeg
1 tablespoon vanilla extract
1 jar (6 ounces) pineapple jam or substitute another fruit jam

Preheat the oven to 350°F. Spray a 10-inch by 15-inch pan with nonstick cooking spray.

Cut the bread into bite-size pieces. In a large mixing bowl, combine the bread with the evaporated and whole milk and set aside for 10 minutes. Beat the eggs thoroughly and add to the bread. Add the remaining ingredients and mix well. Pour into the pan.

Bake for 50 minutes or until lightly browned. Serve warm or cooled.

Cheese Strata

Yield: 24 servings

NANCY M. ALWARD, CHRIST CHURCH, EXETER, NEW HAMPSHIRE

This recipe is easily multiplied. Serve at a brunch accompanied by sliced ham, rolls, and coffee.

48 slices day-old bread, trimmed of all crusts
2 pounds cheddar cheese, thinly sliced
16 eggs
10 cups milk
2 teaspoons prepared mustard
4 tablespoons minced onion
4 teaspoons salt
1/2 teaspoon pepper

Arrange half the bread slices in greased baking dishes 2" deep. Cover with cheese slices. Top with remaining bread. Beat eggs. Add milk, mustard, onion, salt, and pepper, and blend in. Pour over bread and cheese. Refrigerate 1 hour or overnight. Bake uncovered at 325°F for about 50 minutes or until puffy and brown.

Quick Chocolate Cake

Yield: Makes about 100 servings

Patricia A. Johnson, Ladies Aid Society, Gilsum Congregational Church, Gilsum, New Hampshire

A very fudgy and moist cake. Serve with frosting, whipped cream, or ice cream.

4 cups water
1-1/2 cups vegetable oil
1/4 cup vinegar
1-1/2 tablespoons vanilla extract
7 cups all-purpose white flour
3/4 cup unsweetened cocoa powder
4 cups white sugar
1-1/2 tablespoons baking soda
2 tablespoons baking powder
1-1/2 teaspoons salt

Preheat the oven to 350°F. Grease an 18-inch by 26-inch sheet pan.

In a large bowl, combine the water, oil, vinegar, and vanilla. Mix well. In a separate bowl, whisk together the flour, cocoa, sugar, soda, baking powder, and salt. Add the dry ingredients to the wet and mix until smooth. Pour into the prepared pan.

Bake for approximately 45 minutes or until a tester inserted near the center comes out clean. Cool in the pan.

Melba Ice Cream Sauce

Yield: 20 servings

Marguerite R. Curtiss, Women of the Moose (Loyal Order of Moose), Keene, New Hampshire

Served over ice cream or vanilla pudding, this wonderful combination of peach and raspberry is a good way to make a simple dessert really special.

1 jar (10 ounces) peach preserves
1/2 cup raspberry preserves
1/2 cup currant jelly
1/4 cup lemon juice

Combine all the ingredients in a medium-size saucepan. Heat until melted. Stir to blend. Cool.

Helpful Tips

for Putting on a Successful, Traditional New England Church Supper

Choosing a Date

Select your date carefully — check to make sure there are no conflicts, like school vacation or sports events, that will compete for attendance, and then get it on the town calendar early to discourage Johnny-come-latelys from upstaging you.

Menu

Choose do-ahead recipes to minimize last minute preparations. Keep it simple — a simple dish prepared well goes over better than an elaborate dish that's hard to prepare and few will appreciate.

Timeline

Start early, months ahead, and create a timeline of activities that are essential to your success: Set date, book venue, publicity, tickets — printing and advance sales, select and schedule entertainment or speaker, if any, menu, shopping, volunteers, organizing committee, promotion, signs, meal preparation, door ticket sales, table setting, table ware, table decoration.

Committee

Choose your committee wisely. Make sure to include one or two who were closely involved in previous years and one or two new faces who can learn the ropes and carry the tradition forward. Delegate committee tasks so no one person is overwhelmed by the undertaking: Chair, ticket sales — advance and on site, promotion, cooks (chef and prep), shopping, table setting, clean up, table decoration, food runners, entertainment, floater (at the dinner, in charge of keeping an eye out and make sure things run smoothly, filling in as needed).